# A Brief Guide to Writing About Literature

Deborah Barberousse
*Horry-Georgetown Technical College*

HOUGHTON MIFFLIN COMPANY    BOSTON    TORONTO

DALLAS    GENEVA, ILLINOIS    PALO ALTO    PRINCETON, NEW JERSEY

# Contents

# Introduction

At its best, literature is a shared experience. The author shares his or her perspective, attitude, and experience in the writing of the work. In turn, the reader brings his or her own perspective, attitude, and experience to the reading, enjoyment, and interpretation of the work. The result is a blending of worlds and ideas that not only entertains but also enriches our lives as readers and opens new avenues of thought.

Just as an archeologist digs through the ruins of an ancient civilization in order to learn more about it, we, as readers, can discover much about the values, mores, customs, and philosophies of the people of any historical era by reading the literature of that time. As modern-day readers, for example, we can be transported back to ancient Greece through the plays of Sophocles and understand the philosophical and religious views of the citizens of Greece in the fifth century B.C. Unfettered by the shackles of time, Sophocles continues to share with us his world and the world of a people who were once as vital and alive as we are today.

Literature, no matter the time in which it is written, also continues the cycle of shared humanity by dealing with themes of universal concern, themes to which we can all relate. It is this nature of literature that enables it to endure, allowing us to read Sophocles today and, in spite of the differences in his world and ours, to recognize human nature, to recognize ourselves, and to say with a sigh, or perhaps a note of surprise, "Ah, yes. That's how it is."

Someday, somewhere, students will be sitting in classrooms studying the literature of our time. Students just like yourself will be writing essays based on our stories, novels, poems, and plays. By doing so, they will be participating in the sharing, learning about what is important to the people of our time, discovering ways in which we are different and ways in which we are alike. Our world will continue to live on through the literature we pass to them, and they will continue the cycle of sharing by writing about it and, therefore, about us.

But now it is your time to share. When you, as a reader and student, put into writing your interpretation and analysis of a piece of literature, whether an ancient play or a modern-day novel, you set into motion a continuation of the cycle of sharing innate in literature. However, just as you realize that analyzing and interpreting certain literary works can sometimes be difficult, you must also realize that writing about literature requires careful consideration in order that your own analysis be clear and correct. Although there are no guaranteed formulas for writing about literature, there are several tried and true methods and approaches to ensure that you get on the right track and stay there in writing your paper, producing, one hopes, an exciting and enlightening discourse and a continuation of one of the most exciting aspects of literature—sharing.

# CHAPTER ONE

# Preparing to Write

Preparing to write can be just as important, if not more so, than actually writing the paper. Good preparation will simplify the entire writing process and help you write a better paper.

## Choosing What to Write About

Not everyone responds to every literary work alike. Some pieces you will like, others you will not, and some works will leave you ambivalent, just as certain authors will strike a chord with you and others will not. Most teachers, recognizing that writing about literature involves individual student reaction and interpretation, will allow you some freedom in selecting authors, literary works, and topics on which to write. Whenever possible, therefore, you should choose to write about a work of literature that appeals to you, at least on some level.

However, even when you have been assigned a specific author or literary work, it is likely that certain aspects of that author's writing or certain elements within the work will appeal to you more than others. For example, Ernest Hemingway's short story, "Hills Like White Elephants," may not be one of your favorites in terms of theme, but you may be fascinated with the way in which Hemingway uses simplistic prose, allowing the emotion in the story to be communicated almost entirely by the direct actions of the characters. If so, you now have the basis for a paper about literature into which you can sink your teeth.

## Reading Critically

Once you have chosen an author or literary work about which to write, you need to read critically with an eye to anything that calls out as meaningful or significant.

## Marking Passages

One of the best methods of critical reading involves marking passages with a pencil, underlining and making margin notes as you proceed. This method is one of the most effective because it keeps the work and your notations about it directly linked, but it should be used only if the book you are marking is your own.

## Using Index Cards

Another excellent method of critical reading involves using index cards, also referred to as note cards, to note meaningful and significant details. When using note cards, be sure to add page number or line number notations on each card so that you can easily go back to those passages to review them as they relate to the entire work.

Note cards work well because as you begin to write your paper you can shuffle the cards according to the organization of your paper, ensuring that your notes are used well and at the appropriate place in your paper.

## Photocopying

You may photocopy specific passages of a work (not an entire work) for reference, according to copyright laws. Then, as you begin writing your paper, you may choose to mark on the photocopied sheets rather than in the book itself.

Regardless of the method you use for marking, what should you note as you read? The list is endless and to a great extent depends on where you plan to go with your paper. You may have an idea about your thesis before you begin reading critically and marking, or one may begin to form as you look at the work critically.

Some typical notations might include particular use of:

- language
- symbolism
- irony
- structure
- tone
- dialogue
- character
- description
- plot movement
- imagery
- foreshadowing
- epiphany
- theme development

Later, when you have developed a clear and focused thesis for your paper, you can go back over the work and disregard notations that are not significant to your focus. In the meantime, however, you should note anything that strikes you as significant. It is better to mark it now than to have to experience the frustration of digging for something you vaguely remember later. Also, through your notations, you may find that the way to proceed with your paper has spoken for itself.

# CHAPTER TWO

## Approaches

Once you have chosen a literary work and have read it critically, it is important to determine the approach you will take in writing about it. Most literary essays fall into one of three categories of approaches: **explication, analysis, and comparison/contrast.**

Although the approaches differ to a great extent, you will find that all have one element in common: each is written with the intent of showing how the author has carried out or furthered a theme, or message, of the work.

By asking yourself a series of questions about specific literary elements in the work(s) under consideration, you can better discover which elements to discuss in your paper and what approach to take:

1. Are there any **allusions** that seem significant?
2. Are there any **symbols** in the work, and how has the author used **symbolism** to express his or her thoughts? Can any of the symbols be interpreted in different ways?
3. What **images** are particularly strong?
4. Is there any **irony** in the work, and how has the author used irony to express his or her meaning?
5. How has the author used **language** (connotations, figurative language) to express his or her meaning?
6. What is the **tone** of the work, and how is the tone significant to our understanding of the message?
7. Is the **plot structure** of the work significant?
8. When dealing with poetry, is the overall **structure** of the poem significant?
9. Has the author used **foreshadowing** as a part of the structure of the work, and how is the foreshadowing significant?
10. How has the author used **sound** to express his or her thoughts?
11. What is especially significant about the development of the **characters**? Are any minor characters significant in the development of the theme? Have any of the characters experienced an **epiphany**?
12. How is **setting** used in the work?

13. Does the **point of view** from which the work is told play an important role in our understanding of the work?
14. How is **dialogue** used to express the action or meaning?
15. What is the **theme** of the work? Is there more than one major theme?
16. How do any or all of these elements work together to create the meaning?

# Explication

To **explicate** means to explain, and a **theme of explication** involves the explanation of a meaning or meanings in a work of literature.

An essay that is based on this approach moves carefully through a work of literature, or sometimes through a passage or segment of a work, calling attention to details and noting anything and everything meaningful used to further the author's theme. Almost any element of literature can be used in your explication.

Explication works best with poetry. As such, an explication paper on poetry moves through the poem, sometimes line by line, sometimes passage by passage, noting its complexities.

Because explication involves such attention to detail, it generally does not work well as an approach to writing about entire short stories, novels, or plays. Yet works of literature such as these can most certainly benefit from explication when limited to selected passages or scenes. In dealing with these longer works, it is best to identify and explain a particular descriptive passage, a key scene, a conversation, or a monologue. Explication used in this way is an excellent approach to writing about longer works in order to show how minute details in a work contribute dramatically to the whole.

The organization of a theme of explication is the most obvious and simplistic of all the approaches. Since explication involves explaining, it is best to simply begin at the beginning of the work or passage and work through to the end. The organization of the essay essentially follows the organization of the piece of work or the passage.

One final, but important, note about explication must be made. Explication does not mean paraphrasing, or rewording. A paper that simply rewords the author's words, line by line or passage by passage, would not only be boring to the reader but also a colossal insult to the author. Although it may be necessary within the explication to sometimes paraphrase in order to clarify, such paraphrasing should not be the entire basis of the paper.

# Analysis

To **analyze** means to separate a subject into its elements as a means to understanding the whole. A **theme of analysis,** therefore, approaches a work of literature by examining one or several key elements.

An essay that is based on this approach looks not at the entire work in terms of explaining it, but rather at how the author has used one or several elements of literature to carry out or further a theme.

The keys to a well-written analysis paper include a specific focus on the element or elements under discussion and clear organization. Two basic methods of organization work well in analysis:

## One-Element Organization

This organizational method identifies one element or technique used to carry out the theme of the work and develops the paper based on various ways in which that element is used.

## Several Elements Organization

This organizational method identifies several elements or techniques used to carry out the theme of the work and develops the paper based on individual discussion of those elements.

Although there are other methods of organization for an analysis paper, these two patterns work well and can be easily modified to suit the purpose of the paper.

# Comparison/Contrast

To **compare** means to show how two subjects are alike, to **contrast** means to show how two subjects are different, and to **compare and contrast** means to show how two subjects are both alike and different. Therefore, it is feasible that a **comparison/contrast essay** may actually involve any one of three approaches: it may compare, it may contrast, or it may do both.

An essay that is based on the comparison/contrast approach may deal with two subjects within one literary work, two or more works on the same subject or with the same basic theme, two or more works by the same author, two authors and their works, or one work compared or contrasted to a particular style of writing.

As with analysis, the key to a well-written comparison/contrast essay lies in its organization. First, it is important to not only identify the two subjects to be discussed, but to also determine the basis of comparison/contrast.

Generally, it is best to look at several ways in which the subjects can be compared/contrasted. Finding a basis for comparison/contrast isn't as complicated as it might seem. In fact, you do this sort of thing all the time. For example, if you were considering two colleges to attend, you would likely establish a basis of comparison/contrast as you attempted to make your decision. You might compare/contrast the two, for example, on the basis of cost, programs offered, and location. The same is true when using comparison/contrast in literary essays.

It is important for the organization of the paper to clearly identify the manner in which the subjects will be compared/contrasted in order to avoid a discussion that goes in too many directions and is confusing to the reader.

Once the subjects and the basis of comparison/contrast have been identified, a comparison/contrast essay may be organized in one of two basic patterns:

## Block Method

This organizational method first discusses one of the subjects under consideration according to the identified basis of comparison/contrast elements and then discusses the second subject according to the same basis.

## Point by Point Method

This organizational method discusses each of the identified basis of comparison/contrast elements using examples from the two subjects.

A comparison/contrast essay based on literature may seem difficult to pull together; however, these two patterns of organization limit and direct the scope of your essay, resulting in a clearly stated, logical discussion.

Because of the nature of comparison/contrast, you will find that this approach to writing works well whether you are considering short stories, novels, poetry, or drama.

Just as you have preferences in reading literature, you will find that you also have preferences in approaches to writing about literature. Also, although your paper should follow one basic approach, it is certainly possible that one or both of the other approaches will be included within the paper. For example, it is entirely acceptable for a comparison/contrast paper to include some explication as well as some analysis, just as an analysis paper may include some explication and some comparison/contrast.

Obviously, approach it important. However, the writing approach should not dictate the choice of literature. Instead, the literature under discussion should dictate the choice of approach. Therefore, critical reading of the literature you intend to write about can lead you to ask some pertinent questions about the work(s) in general, besides the questions you have asked about individual literary elements. Your answers may further point to the direction and approach you should take in your paper. For example:

1. How have the author's own life experiences affected the work of literature he or she has created?
2. Is there some particular historical significance to the work? Does it show us something about a specific time or place?
3. Can we compare the work of one author with that of another author writing on the same subject? Can we find a basis of comparison or contrast for two or more works by the same author?
4. Does the work set forth some universal theme of love, death, or human nature?

None of these questions and the approaches they may lead to are intended to constrict your creativity and imagination. Rather, they serve as guidelines and patterns that can and should be modified to suit your purpose and the literary work(s) under discussion.

# CHAPTER THREE
## The Process

Writing a paper based on literature is no different in form than writing any other type of essay. As you know, most essays are based on a three-part structure:

- an introduction with a thesis statement
- a body made up of several supporting paragraphs
- a conclusion

Each part of an essay needs to follow general guidelines in order to ensure clear and effective organization. By asking yourself a series of questions concerning the structure of your paper, you can check yourself to see that you have followed those guidelines.

## The Introduction and Thesis Statement

1. Have I started my discussion of the topic in fairly broad terms rather than jumping right into my thesis statement?
2. Does my introduction identify the work(s) of literature to be discussed and the author(s)?
3. Has my introduction proceeded to narrow the focus more and more until it has reached a clear and narrow thesis statement?
4. Does my thesis statement express the controlling idea of the essay?
5. Is my thesis stated in one tightly focused sentence, and is it located near the end of the paragraph?

## The Body

1. Have I selected an appropriate number of main points to effectively support my thesis, and have I developed one point per paragraph?

2. Have I developed clear support for my thesis through each body paragraph?
3. Have I adhered to the standards of good paragraph writing in each paragraph, and does each have a clearly focused topic sentence?
4. Has each body paragraph explained (explication approach), analyzed (analysis approach), or compared/contrasted (comparison/contrast approach) the work(s) and/or author(s) under discussion, according to the approach I have selected?
5. If I am using the explication approach, has the organization of the body of my paper followed the organization of the work or passage itself?
6. If I am using the analysis or comparison/contrast approach, have I saved my strongest point for the last body paragraph?
7. Have I supported the topic of each paragraph with material from the work(s) under discussion?
8. Does the body of my paper have continuity, and does it flow logically from one point to the next, employing good transition?

## The Conclusion

1. Have I started the concluding paragraph with the general idea of my thesis?
2. Have I avoided simply restating the thesis?
3. Have I used the concluding paragraph to summarize or to draw a conclusion based on my thesis and on the body paragraphs?
4. Have I worked toward a more generalized discussion of the topic near the end of my conclusion?

In addition to ensuring a clear organization, these checklists can also help you maintain the focus of your essay and enable you to create an effective, logical discussion.

# CHAPTER FOUR
## Documentation

One of the areas that concerns student writers the most when writing about literature involves how to use quotes from the work(s) or author(s). Although documentation of references to sources is not a difficult process, it is a critical part of writing your paper and must be handled according to accepted standards.

Most teachers prefer that literary papers use **MLA documentation style,** which sets forth standardization of references to sources. Although other documentation styles exist, MLA is universally accepted within the humanities. Many composition and literature textbooks contain a section on MLA documentation, and most college bookstores sell manuscript documentation booklets. If you do not have a copy of the MLA documentation guidelines, you need to obtain one before writing a literary paper.

## Use of Quotations and Paraphrasing

Although MLA guidelines are quite specific and complete, a few points are especially important to remember.

- You must give credit to all sources you use (cite), including the work(s) under discussion, by using parenthetical documentation within the paper and including a Works Cited page at the end.
- You should integrate paraphrases and quotations with your own discussion and interpretation.
- You should use direct quotations when it is important that you reproduce the words exactly as they are written so as not to lose something vital. Otherwise, you should paraphrase.
- Quotations of less than four lines of your paper should be worked into your essay as any other sentence, followed by parenthetical documentation. Be sure to use quotation marks to indicate directly quoted material.

- Quotations that will take more than four lines of your paper should be set off by indenting ten spaces from the left margin. Such quotations should be double-spaced like the rest of the paper, not single-spaced as some older documentation styles indicate. Do not use quotation marks, but follow the quote with parenthetical documentation.

## Parenthetical Documentation

The MLA guidelines include instruction in how to cite references within the paper using **parenthetical documentation.** Parenthetical documentation simply refers to a set of parentheses containing identification of the source coming after the cited material.

Each literary form—fiction, poetry, and drama—uses different parenthetical reference forms. It's important that you recognize the correct documentation format for each and apply it correctly.

- When citing a passage from a short story or novel, indicate the page number.

   Example: "It is impossible to say how first the idea entered my brain; but once conceived, it haunted me day and night" (37).

- When citing a part of a poem, indicate the line number(s).

   Example: "The only other sound's the sweep/Of easy wind and downy flake" (11–13).

   *Note:* When quoting lines from poetry, a slash (/) is used to indicate the end of a line as it is printed.

- When citing a part of a classic play, indicate the act, scene, and line numbers.

   Example: "There are more things in heaven and earth, Horatio,/Than are dreamt of in your philosophy" (I.v.166–167).

   *Note:* If the play you are citing is a classic verse play, a slash (/) is used to indicate the end of a line as it is printed. If it is not a verse play, no slashes are used.

- When citing a part of a modern play, indicate the act and page number.

   Example: "I am not a dime a dozen! I am Willy Loman, and you are Biff Loman" (II.1421).

- If you are using more than one source for your paper, such as two poems, you will need to use more detailed parenthetical information, according to MLA guidelines, or you will need to indicate in the text of your paper which source you are referring to in order to avoid confusion.

> Example: In "Stopping by Woods on a Snowy Evening," Frost describes the quiet of an evening in the country by explaining "The only other sound's the sweep/Of easy wind and downy flake" (11–13). In contrast, the city nights speak more loudly. Frost explains in "Acquainted With the Night" that he has ". . . stood still and stopped the sound of feet/ When far away an interrupted cry/Came over houses from another street" (7–9).

# Works Cited Page

Also included in the MLA guidelines is instruction in how to document your sources on a Works Cited page. The Works Cited page comes at the end of your paper and lists all the sources you have used.

Technically speaking, your essay should conclude with a Works Cited page listing all the sources you have used according to MLA style. However, if you have used only one source, such as your textbook, your teacher may prefer that you use simple parenthetical references as described above and omit the Works Cited page. If in doubt, you should ask your teacher which method he or she prefers.

# Smooth Use of Quotes

It's important that your quotes from the work(s) under discussion be worked into your paper smoothly. This can best be accomplished by weaving a quote in as a part of your own sentence. However, keep in mind that when you do so, you may need to use only part of the material you are quoting in order to create correct sentence form and correct verb or pronoun agreement. This can be accomplished by using ellipsis marks—three spaced periods to indicate words omitted from a quotation (as in the correct example below).

Also, it is not a good idea to simply quote a passage and then follow it with a sentence telling what the passage means. Instead, try to work the quote in along with your explanation.

> Incorrect: "I put my forehead down to the damp, seaweed-smelling sand" (2). This is an example of Robert Bly's metaphorical language in his poem "In Rainy September."

Correct:   Robert Bly uses metaphorical language in his poem "In
           Rainy September" when he describes how he put his fore-
           head ". . . down to the damp, seaweed-smelling sand" (2).

Correct documentation is an integral part of writing about literature. Documentation style has been greatly simplified over the years, and using it correctly is not difficult. However, careful attention must be paid to correct documentation in order to avoid plagiarism and to avoid confusion for the
reader.

# CHAPTER FIVE
## Writing About Stories or Novels

If you plan to write a literary paper based on a short story or novel, you should read the story or novel thoroughly and carefully, all the while noting your overall reaction and trying to determine the author's message. Critical reading will help you determine the point you want to make in your paper and, in turn, the approach you will take.

Because of the lengthy nature of most short stories and novels, explication may not be the best approach, unless you plan to explicate selected passages in order to make your point. However, analysis and comparison/contrast work quite well as approaches to writing about short stories and novels.

Whether you choose to use explication, analysis, or comparison/contrast for your paper about a short story or novel, some key elements for consideration include:

- plot
- characters
- setting
- point of view

- symbolism
- irony
- them
- tone

## Sample Student Essay

The following student essay is based on Jose Donoso's short story, "Paseo," and uses analysis as an approach. It takes into account how one element of a short story, symbolism, can be interpreted in several ways in order to create the whole.

The organization of the essay is set up so that each body paragraph analyzes a different interpretation of a single symbol:

1. Introduction and Thesis: Jose Donoso's short story, "Paseo," uses multiple interpretations of a single symbol, the dog.
2. The dog representing emotion

Jane Perry

English 102, Section 1

Ms. Barberousse

December 11, 1992

The Object of Her Affections

The use of symbolism has long been a technique by which an author can present far more than the literal meaning of a story. However, symbols are not always easily defined; indeed, it is sometimes possible that one symbol in a story may be endowed with multiple meanings, all of which lead the reader to a greater understanding of the author's message. Such is the case in Jose Donoso's short story, "Paseo." The story is told from the point of view of a grown man looking back on the isolated, frightened child he was. As the boy's jealousy focuses on the attention gained by a nondescript but persistent dog, Donoso leads us into the realm of multiple symbolism.

Perhaps most obviously, the dog represents emotion. The boy in the story grows up with cold people in a house that is "not happy" (316) and that expresses "an absence, a lack, which because it was unacknowledged was irremediable" (316). The boy wishes for more from his family. "I wished," he tells us, "that their confined feeling might overflow and express itself in a fit of rage, for example, or with some bit of

foolery" (317). Of course, he knows it is not to be. The dog
that his Aunt Mathilda adopts, however, represents the oppo-
site of repressed, or perhaps nonexistent, emotion. "Her whole
body, from her quivering snout to her tail ready to waggle,
was full of an abundant capacity for fun" (323). It is the
dog's expression of emotion that permeates Aunt Mathilda's
cold exterior and provokes her to express emotion of her own.
Yet, still, the boy is isolated, perhaps more so, as his jealousy takes hold. As he watches his aunt stroke the dog sleep-
ing on her lap, he realizes the extent of his own isolation
and feels the loss of any hope that he, too, might be the re-
cipient of her affection:

> On seeing that expressionless hand reposing there, I no-
> ticed that the tension which had kept my aunt's features
> clenched before, relented, and that a certain peace was
> now softening her face. I could not resist. I drew closer
> to her on the sofa, as if to a newly kindled fire. I hoped
> that she would reach out to me with a look or include me
> with a smile. But she did not (324).

In addition to emotion, the dog also represents disorder
and its effect on constrained order. Dedicated to her broth-
ers, one of whom is the father of the boy in the story, Aunt
Mathilda is the creator of order in the house, one whose focus
is frightening in its rigidity and in her insistence on per-

fection. Defects cannot be tolerated and, as the boy relates, ". . . when she saw affliction about her she took immediate steps to remedy what, without doubt, were errors in a world that should be, that had to be, perfect" (317). Yet, with the dog's appearance there are "things that can neither be explained nor resolved" (319). The dog itself is a walking representation of disorder:

> It was small and white, with legs which were too short for its size and an ugly pointed snout that proclaimed an entire genealogy of misalliances: the sum of unevenly matched breeds which for generations had been scouring the city, searching for food in the garbage cans and among the refuse of the port (320).

Mathilda, surprisingly, grows more and more attached to the dog, and with her attachment comes the beginning of chaos. The chaos starts with simple things, such as Mathilda losing at billiards and no longer remembering the order of the shooters, but it progresses to the point that she loses "the thread of order" (323) that has been the thread of her life. Eventually, the disorder so dissolves the very core of Mathilda that her midnight strolls extend to her disappearance.

In retrospect, the dog also represents madness, a madness that results when the spontaneity of the dog disrupts the rigid world of the adults. The boy speculates on the first

look that passes between the dog and his aunt and feels that
look "contained some secret commitment" (320), and her
half-hearted attempt to make the dog go away seems "a last ef-
fort to repel an encroaching destiny" (320). When the dog
first makes Mathilda laugh, the boy is surprised, but not
amused, because he ". . . may have felt the dark thing that
had stirred it up" (324). It is that unnamed dark thing that
permeates the boy's jealousy and causes him to imagine a sin-
ister influence in the dog. When he perceives in his aunt "an
animation in her eyes, an excited restlessness like that in
the eyes of the animal" (326) after one of her evening walks
with the dog, the boy begins to feel concern rather than jealousy. His aunt, formerly a fortress of routine and order, has
become a mystery of the night:

> Those two were accomplices. The night protected them. They
> belonged to the murmuring sound of the city, to the sirens
> of the ships which, crossing the dark or illuminated
> streets, the houses and factories and parks, reached my
> ears (326).

One night upon hearing his aunt come in, the boy recognizes the final influence the dog and the madness it represents are to have on his aunt. "I went to bed terrified, knowing this was the end. I was not mistaken. Because one night

. . . Aunt Mathilda took the dog out for a walk after dinner, and did not return" (327).

Who is to say whether the aunt's disappearance is a manifestation of her madness or simply a rebellion on her part, an affirmation of the life she has never before experienced? Yet, in the boy's mind, she is dead, and her death has been brought about by the dog and all it symbolizes. The repression of emotion in his aunt has been freed by something not human, and in doing so it has brought disorder to order and madness to composure.

Works Cited

Donoso, Jose. "Paseo." The Riverside Anthology of Literature.

    Ed. Douglas Hunt. 2nd ed. Boston: Houghton Mifflin, 1991.

    315-327.

# CHAPTER SIX
## Writing About Poetry

Poetry is perhaps the oldest form of literature known to humankind. It has been used throughout the ages as a form of history, an expression of religion, and a presentation of images and emotions. Whatever its form, however, poetry is intended to create in us the experience that is being expressed.

Because poetry, by nature, is so rich in language and its subtleties, it lends itself to all three literary essay approaches. Explication, for example, provides an excellent opportunity to explore the artistry and talent involved in employing a wide range of elements and techniques to create the whole. Analysis, too, is an excellent approach for a paper based on poetry, where the discussion is narrowed to just one or several basic elements or techniques. Also, it is quite typical to find poetry the basis of comparison/contrast papers in terms of subject, theme, and authors.

Some key elements to consider when writing about poetry, whether you are explicating, analyzing, or comparing/contrasting, include:

- speaker
- sound
- imagery
- figures of speech
- connotations

- symbolism
- irony
- structure
- tone
- theme

## Sample Student Essay

The following student essay is based on Louise Bogan's poem, "The Dream," and uses explication as an approach. The organization of the essay is a simple one, following the organization of the poem itself, as explication should. It takes into account how all the elements of the poem work toward carrying out the theme.

The organization of the essay is set up to take into consideration the four stanzas of the poem and an overall structural discussion:

1. Introduction and Thesis: Louise Bogan's poem, "The Dream," is about fear, and Bogan's message, the message of the dream, in fact, is that fear can be tamed through trust.
2. First stanza
3. Second stanza
4. Third stanza
5. Fourth stanza
6. Overall technical structure
7. Conclusion

Marvin Poplin

English 102, Section 1

Ms. Barberousse

December 4, 1992

Taming the Beast

Dreams have long been the basis for extensive analysis, their meanings interpreted and reinterpreted. Some people believe that dreams reflect our repressed emotions, providing a necessary outlet for the negative aspects of our reality. Others find answers through dreams, believing that dreams provide simple solutions to seemingly complex issues in our lives. Louise Bogan, in her poem, "The Dream," describes a dream that expresses both repression and solution. It is a poem about fear, and Bogan's message, the message of the dream, in fact, is that fear can be tamed through trust.

In the first stanza of the poem the speaker describes the fearful dream she had. Bogan introduces the symbol of a mighty horse that embodies the fear and retribution carried from the speaker's childhood, fear and retribution that have been "... kept for thirty-five years..." (3). Bogan effectively uses metaphorical language as she describes the fear personified in the horse as it "... poured through his mane" (3) and the retribution as it "... breathed through his nose" (4). The source

of her fear is unclear, but it may be that the horse is a symbol of life that can be both beautiful and terrifying. The
imagery created when the speaker tells us, "... the terrible
horse began/To paw at the air, and make for me with his blows"
(1-2) describes a sense of entrapment as life corners her and
spews forth the repressed fear and retribution, emotions that
must be faced.

The speaker's shame at her cowardice is clear in the second stanza as she describes how she "... lay on the ground and
wept" (5). It is at this point that Bogan introduces another
symbol in the poem, a woman who "... leapt for the rein" (6).
The stranger's strength and courage seem so alien to the
speaker that she refers to her as a "creature" (6), something
not shackled by human fears. Perhaps this other woman represents the speaker's alter ego, a side of her yet to be set
free. Nonetheless, Bogan creates a dramatic contrast between
the speaker's inability to respond to her fear as she "lay
half in a swound" (7) and the other woman's determination as
she "Leapt in the air, and clutched at the leather and chain"
(8).

In the third stanza, the other woman advises the speaker
to give the horse a token as a gesture of peace. "Throw him,
she said, some poor thing you alone claim" (9). In effect, she
tells the speaker to surrender to her fate and to approach

life with love. The speaker's long-held sense of hopelessness
and fear is further contrasted to the possibility of a fresh
approach to life as she tells the stranger, "... No, no ... he
hates me; he's out for harm,/And whether I yield or not, it is
all the same" (11-12).

Yet, face to face with her fears, perhaps shamed by the
courage of the other woman, the speaker yields at last in the
final stanza of the poem. The imagery created is one of coldness, the coldness that resides in the heart of fear. She describes her act of courage and the fear still inherent in that
act when she explains, "... I flung the glove/Pulled from my
sweating, my cold right hand" (14-15). With that act, the
imagery changes from cold to warmth as suddenly as does the
beast who, like life that "... no one may understand" (15),
came to her side and "... put down his head in love" (16). After thirty-five years, the beast is tamed.

Like dreams so often are, Bogan's poem is a simple one,
not only in the narration of the dream, but also in the metrical pattern and the rhyme scheme of the poem. Rarely is a reg-
ular iambic beat achieved in the poem, thus reinforcing the
theme of confusion. Yet, at the end of the poem, when the
meaning is clear, the last line contains three successive
iambs in "put down his head in love." Also, after a routine
rhyme scheme of abab in the first three stanzas, Bogan intro-

duces new tension in the last stanza with an abba rhyme scheme. The word "love" comes fresh and unexpectedly to rhyme with "glove," just as Bogan's poem points out that with trust comes peace, often just as fresh and unexpectedly.

Louise Bogan points out in her poem that life is rarely as predictable as we might like, but it must be faced, regardless of our fears. Like the speaker, we may be surprised by the gentleness and peace we find when we face life head on, offer it our love, and surrender to its power—just as it surrenders to ours.

Works Cited

Bogan, Louise. "The Dream." The Riverside Anthology of Litera-

ture. Ed. Douglas Hunt. 2nd ed. Boston: Houghton Mifflin,

1991. 730.

# CHAPTER SEVEN
## Writing About Drama

Since its ancient beginnings, drama has been used as a literary vehicle to express the plight of humankind in conflict with their world. Through the unfolding of events in a play, human existence is played out through a cause and effect relationship. However, the biggest difference between drama and other forms of literature is that drama is intended to be seen as it is acted out on a stage, a fact that is critical to interpretation as a play is read.

As is true with short stories and novels, explication may not be the best approach for your literary paper about drama unless you plan to explicate a key scene, a conversation, or a monologue. Used in this way, explication can be an excellent approach to show how minute details in a play contribute dramatically to the whole. Analysis works quite well as an approach to writing about drama since it is possible to analyze how a single element or several elements within the large body of work are used to set forth a specific theme. Theme also serves as an excellent starting point for the comparison/contrast approach to drama, whether expressed historically or through character. An essay based on drama may typically include a discussion of one or several of the following basic elements:

- dialogue
- plot
- characters
- conflict
- setting
- symbolism
- dramatic conventions
- theme

## Sample Student Essay

The following student essay is based on Aristotle's definition of tragedy and Arthur Miller's play, *Death of a Salesman*. The paper uses a comparison approach. Although Miller's play is a modern one, when compared to the concept of Aristotelian tragedy, it can be viewed as adhering to the basic definition.

The organization of the essay is set up according to the point-by-point method, using each of Aristotle's defining points of tragedy as a basis of comparison:

1. Introduction and Thesis: Arthur Miller's great twentieth-century tragedy, *Death of a Salesman,* in spite of its modernity, can be successfully compared to the Aristotelian description of traditional tragedy.
2. The tragic hero
3. The hero's tragic flaw
4. The hero's recognition of the truth about himself
5. Redemption
6. Conclusion

Della Smith

English 102, Section 1

Ms. Barberousse

December 1, 1992

*Death of a Salesman*: A Modern Tragedy

In the fourth century B.C., Aristotle set forth his description of dramatic tragedy, and for centuries after, tragedy continued to be defined by his basic observations. It wasn't until the modern age that playwrights began to deviate somewhat from the basic tenets of Aristotelian tragedy, and, in doing so, began to create plays more recognizable to the common people and, thereby, less traditional. Even so, upon examination, the basic plot structure of some modern tragedy actually differs very little from that of the ancient classics. Arthur Miller's great twentieth-century tragedy, *Death of a Salesman*, in spite of its modernity, can be successfully compared to the Aristotelian description of traditional tragedy.

According to Aristotle, the protagonist, or tragic hero, of a tragedy is a person of great virtue and of high estate, usually a member of a royal family. The tragedy then carries the protagonist from his position of esteem and happiness to one of misery. Although Miller's protagonist, Willy Loman, is not of high estate, he is the head of his household. His wife, Linda, aware though she is of his failings, sees him as "... the dearest man in the world ..." (I.1373). Furthermore, he is a man whose intentions to be the best salesman possible are honorable, although misguided. It must not be overlooked that prior to the twentieth century, almost all literature had as its protagonist someone of high estate. The typical protagonist of the modern age, however, is one whose main conflict is survival, and that conflict is certainly true of Willy Loman. Linda summarizes the plight of the modern tragic hero when she says, "A small man can be just as exhausted as a great man" (I.1374).

Aristotelian tragedy further defines the tragic hero as one who has a tragic flaw or frailty that is very often the error of pride. It is this tragic flaw that causes the hero's downfall. Willy Loman's tragic flaw is certainly bound by his pride, a pride that will not allow him to recognize that he is not the salesman he has always dreamed of being. As a result, he becomes further and further detached from reality, believing more in his dreams than in reality. When Linda tries to get Willy to slow down his travels and work in New York, he tells her, "I'm the New England man. I'm vital in New England" (I.1347). Yet, Willy has just returned from another unsuccessful New England sales trip. His pride will also not allow him to recognize that he is no longer respected by his sons, nor have they become the great successes he has dreamed of for them. When Biff, Willy's older son, momentarily falls for his brother's sporting goods business scheme, Willy tells them, "I see great things for you kids, I think your troubles are over. But remember, start big and you'll end big" (I.1379).

The Aristotelian hero eventually recognizes the dark truth to his life. With this recognition comes, both for the hero and the audience, further recognition that the downfall has resulted from acts for which he is responsible. After all, the hero is capable of making choices. Willy, too, is capable of making choices, but as Biff states in the Requiem, "He had the wrong dreams. All, all wrong" (1425). As Willy seems to slip further and further from reality toward the end of the play, he actually comes closer to the truth about himself than ever before. In his delusionary discussion with his brother Ben, Willy plans his suicide, and Ben mentions that it might be seen as cowardly. Willy replies, "Why? Does it take more guts to stand here the rest of my life ringing up a zero" (II.1417). Even though he quickly slips back to his destructive pride, the mirror has been faced and Willy has seen a zero. His very act of suicide indicates that he knows he cannot regain the respect of Biff nor can he provide for his fam-

ily, as he has pretended for so long. It is only through his
death that he can make something of himself for them.

Traditional tragic heroes find a form of redemption in
their suffering, and through that suffering, the audience
learns moral lessons and experiences a katharsis. Perhaps
Willy is most notably a true tragic hero in that his tragic
flaw, his battle to be what he is not, is one that is carried
out wrongly but for all the right reasons, as is typical of
the traditional tragic hero. Traditional heroes are also victims to some degree, victims of their own flaw and victims of
a force greater than themselves. In Willy's case, his destructive pride in being what he is not comes about, at least in
part, based on misguided definitions of success. Biff tries to
stop Willy's spiraling fall as he pleads with his father to
"... take that phony dream and burn it before something hap-
pens" (II.1422). However, Willy's definition of success has
been too wrapped up in money for too long. As audience members
of traditional tragedies experience a katharsis, so does Biff,
as he learns from his father's mistakes and realizes that the
key to success lies in knowing who he is. Perhaps it is only
through Biff's recognition of the truth that Willy is re-
deemed, though not as he planned. Biff asks Willy, "Why am I
trying to become what I don't want to be ... when all I want

is out there, waiting for me the minute I say I know who I am"
(II.1421).

Tragedy did not end with the modern age. Instead, it has
found new form and is perhaps more recognizable with the common man as its protagonist. Traditional tragedy is intended to
create in the audience pity and terror for the tragic hero's
condition. Most of us see enough of ourselves in Willy that we
sympathize with him, even when we disagree with him. Furthermore, it is difficult for late-twentieth-century Americans not
to feel terror when considering how the forces that destroyed
Willy might destroy us as well. Perhaps that fear is, indeed,
the very heart of the tragedy Arthur Miller created.

Works Cited

Miller, Arthur. *Death of a Salesman*. The Riverside Anthology

of Literature. Ed. Douglas Hunt. 2nd ed. Boston: Houghton

Mifflin, 1991. 1345-1426.

# CHAPTER EIGHT

# Getting It Right

Although writing about literature is just like any other form of expository writing, certain conventions, or standards, must be considered. These conventions ensure that you make your point clearly with appropriate references to sources and with adherence to specific style guidelines (MLA).

## Literary Essay Conventions

- Use the present tense when discussing works of literature and events within those works.
- Use the past tense only when discussing events that have happened in the past, whether in the author's life or in the story itself.
- Work quotations into your paper smoothly, conforming to correct sentence structure and grammatical form. Quotations should not be overlong nor should they intrude upon the text of your paper; instead, they should become a part of the text, acting as support for your points.
- Use parenthetical documentation for all quotes and include a Works Cited page, according to MLA documentation style.
- Identify works of literature correctly: titles of novels and plays should be underlined; titles of short stories and poems should be enclosed within quotation marks.
- Avoid contractions and colloquialisms.
- Write objectively, avoiding reference to yourself. Expressions such as, "I think," "In my opinion," and "I believe" tend to weaken your point. Your essay is, by its very nature, an expression of your opinion, supported with specific and concrete references to the work.

Once you are assured that you have adhered to the conventions of literary essays in your paper, it is important that you proofread and edit for clarity and correctness.

## Editing Guidelines

- Review your essay to determine if your thesis is narrow enough and that it states something other than the obvious.
- Make sure your basic organization is one that fully and logically develops your thesis.
- Make sure that you have supported each of your main points with specific and concrete references from the work(s) under discussion.
- Check your documentation style according to MLA standards.
- Edit for grammar, spelling, or typing errors.

## Manuscript Form

Correct manuscript form is also an important consideration as you prepare your essay. Again, the standards of MLA documentation style apply to correct manuscript form; however, it is always a good idea to ask your instructor how he or she prefers you to handle issues such as typing, whether or not to have a title page, and whether or not you need to include a Works Cited page.

Although manuscript form is covered in detail by MLA standards, some critical points to consider include the following:

- If you use a title page, it should contain:

  The title of your paper, typed in upper and lower case letters, without quotation marks surrounding it, and without underlining. (Of course, if your title includes the title of the literary work, quotation marks or underlining should be used to indicate the title of the work.)

  Your name

  Your instructor's name, the title of the course, and the date

- If you are not using a title page:

  Identifying information is placed in the upper left-hand corner of the paper's first page. This information begins one inch from the top of the page. The title is centered two spaces below the last line of the identifying information.

The writer's last name and the page number appear in the upper right-hand corner, one-half inch from the top. No words, abbreviations, or punctuation marks are used between the name and the page number.

- Pages after the first page contain the writer's last name and page number one-half inch from the top of the page, and the text begins one inch from the top.

- One-inch margins are used throughout the paper, and all text should be double-spaced.

- Works of literature must be identified correctly in your text by underlining titles of novels and plays and setting titles of short stories and poems within quotation marks.

Your finished paper will be one that allows you to continue the rich heritage of sharing inherent in the study of literature. By participating in this heritage, you may provide fresh insight for future students of literature by adding your perspective to that of those who have come before you.

# Glossary

**Allusion**    An indirect reference to another work of art, a person, or an event.

**Analysis**    A method by which a subject is separated into its elements as a means to understanding the whole. A theme of analysis, therefore, approaches a work of literature by examining one or several key elements.

**Character**    An imagined person used in a work of fiction, poetry, or drama.

**Characterization**    The method by which characters in a work of literature are made known to the reader.

**Comparison**    A discussion concerning how two or more persons or things are alike.

**Conflict**    A struggle among opposing forces in a literary work.

**Connotation**    The set of implications and associations a word carries regardless of its literal meaning.

**Contrast**    A discussion concerning how two or more persons or things are different.

**Dialogue**    Conversation between characters in literature.

**Drama**    A play.

**Dramatic Conventions**    Customary methods of presenting an action using devices that an audience is willing to accept.

**Epiphany**    A moment of insight in a character when that character suddenly knows something about life or about himself or herself previously unrecognized.

**Explication**    A method of explaining. A theme of explication involves the explanation of a meaning or meanings in a work of literature.

**Fiction**    Stories that are at least partially imagined and not factual.

**Figures of Speech**    Words that mean, in a particular context, something more than the dictionary definitions.

**Foreshadowing**    An indication, or hint, of something yet to come.

**Imagery**    The use of words or groups of words that refer to the senses and sensory experiences.

**Irony**   An effect created with statements or situations that seem at odds with how things truly are.

**Metaphor**   An implicit comparison of a feeling or object with another unlike it. Example: He is a snake in the grass.

**Metaphorical Language**   Language that draws comparisons between things that are essentially unalike. Metaphorical language is most often created through the use of metaphor, simile, and personification.

**MLA Documentation Style**   A standardization of references to sources established by the Modern Language Association. Although other documentation styles exist, MLA is universally accepted within the humanities.

**Monologue**   An extended speech by one character in a literary work.

**Narrator**   The person telling the story in a work of literature.

**Novel**   A long fictional narrative.

**Paraphrase**   A restatement in our own words of what we understand a poem or a passage from another form of literature to say.

**Parenthetical Documentation**   A set of parentheses containing identification of the source coming after cited material.

**Personification**   A figure of speech in which nonhuman things are given human characteristics. Example: The car died on the hill.

**Plot**   The planned sequence of events in a literary work.

**Poetry**   A form of writing in which the author writes in lines using either a metrical pattern or free verse.

**Point of View**   The identification of the narrator of a literary work and the limits placed upon the narration.

**Prose**   Any form of writing that is not poetry.

**Setting**   The background upon which a literary work takes place, including the time, place, historical era, geography, and culture.

**Short Story**   A brief fictional narrative. The short story was created and defined in the United States early in the nineteenth century.

**Simile**   A comparison of a feeling or object with another unlike it, using the term "like" or "as." Example: He eats like a horse.

**Summary**   A brief condensation of the main idea of a literary work.

**Symbol**   Something concrete representing something abstract.

**Symbolism**   The use of symbols to give a literary work a message greater than its literal meaning.

**Theme**   The message, or main idea, of a literary work.

**Tone**   The expression of a writer's attitude toward a subject in a literary work and the creation of a mood for that work.